CODE MONKEYS

Debugging

BY JOHN WOOD

BookLife
PUBLISHING

©2020
BookLife Publishing Ltd.
King's Lynn
Norfolk PE30 4LS

A catalogue record for this book is available from the British Library.

ISBN: 978-1-83927-116-8

Written by:
John Wood

Edited by:
Madeline Tyler

Designed by:
Danielle Webster-Jones

IMAGE CREDITS

Images are courtesy of Shutterstock.com. With thanks to Getty Images, Thinkstock Photo and iStockphoto. Cover & throughout – Ori Artiste. 2 – Ann679. 4 – Ann679, GoodStudio, SK Design, feelplus. 5 – ppart. 6 – Robert Kneschke. 7 – Macrovector. 8–9 – Ann679, VectorKnight. 10 – Dean Drobot. 11 – 1000s_pixels, PrinceOfLove. 12 – Kotofonya. 13 – Courtesy of the Naval Surface Warfare Center, Dahlgren, VA., 1988. [Public domain], Marish. 14 – Bakhtiar Zein. 15 – tynyuk. 17 – irin-k. 18 – Nadia Snopek. 19 – ajt. 22 – Ann679 Additional illustration by Danielle Webster-Jones.

Scratch is a project of the Scratch Foundation, in collaboration with the Lifelong Kindergarten Group at the MIT Media Lab. It is available for free at https://scratch.mit.edu

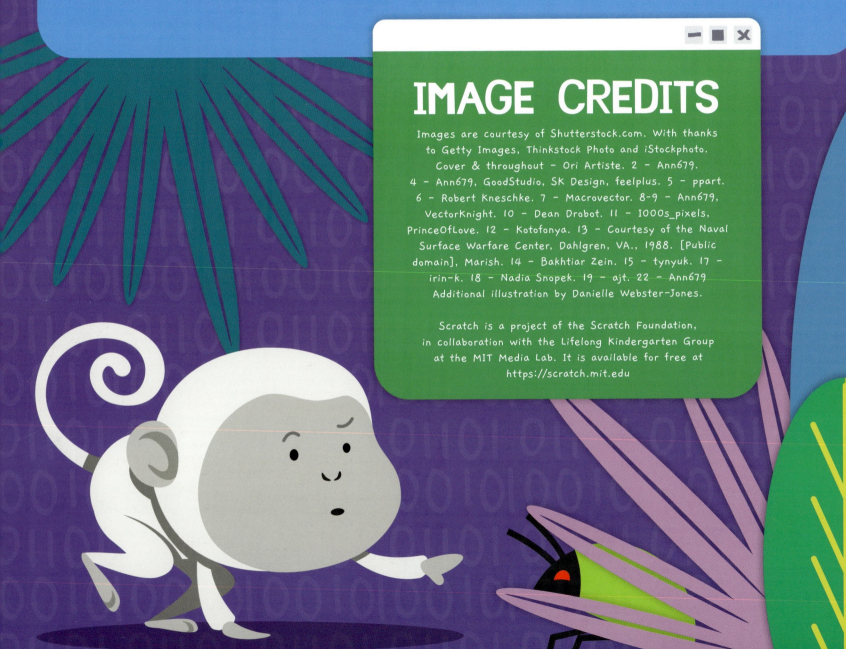

Contents

Words that look like **this** can be found in the glossary on page 24.

Welcome
TO THE JUNGLE

A code monkey is a curious, clever little thing. It wants to know all about computers and coding. Let's follow the code monkeys and learn about coding too!

A code monkey can also be very annoying sometimes. Hey — don't eat that mouse!

FIRST THINGS FIRST

COMPUTER

a machine that can carry out <u>instructions</u>

CODING

writing a set of instructions, called code, to tell computers what to do

PROGRAMMER

a person who writes code (like a human code monkey)

Computers are everywhere. Desktops, laptops, smartphones and tablets are all computers. There are even computers in surprising places, from fridges to lampposts.

Coding
IN THE WILD

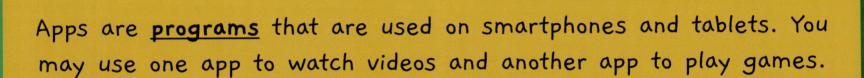

Apps are **programs** that are used on smartphones and tablets. You may use one app to watch videos and another app to play games.

There are millions and millions of apps to choose from.

Every app is built out of code. If an app breaks, the programmer must fix it. Today we will learn how programmers find out what is wrong with their code. It is called debugging.

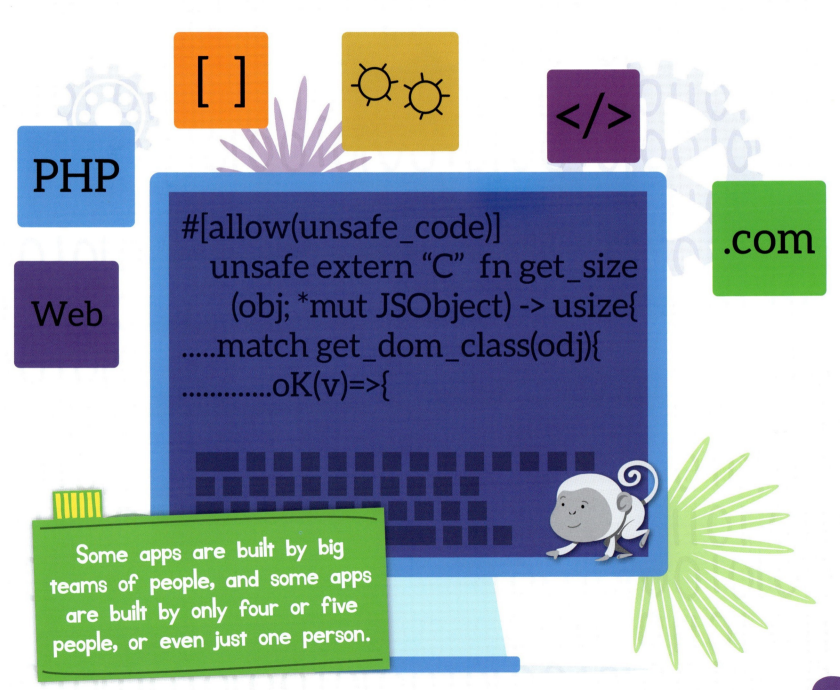

```
#[allow(unsafe_code)]
    unsafe extern "C" fn get_size
    (obj; *mut JSObject) -> usize{
.....match get_dom_class(odj){
..............oK(v)=>{
```

PHP

Web

[ ]

</>

.com

Some apps are built by big teams of people, and some apps are built by only four or five people, or even just one person.

WHAT ARE Bugs?

Silly monkeys! Stop looking for creepy, crawly bugs. In coding, a bug is a part of a code that doesn't work as it should. Bugs are annoying problems that have to be fixed.

Some bugs cause an app or a program to **crash** and stop working. Other bugs just change how a program or app **behaves**. A bug could cause a computer to keep making the same mistakes.

Somebody help this poor computer!

SILLY Computers

It isn't the computer's fault it has a bug – it is the programmer's fault! Computers can't think for themselves like humans and monkeys do. They just follow instructions.

Computers read code, not minds.

Bugs can be caused when the programmer accidentally types the code in incorrectly. Bugs can also be caused if the programmer doesn't realise what their code will really do.

Warning message

Error!

Cancel

11

FIND THOSE Bugs!

Programmers go through their code and look for mistakes. This is called debugging. Debugging can be quite difficult – bugs are hard to find.

Debugging can take a long time.

Even the best programmers can't write the perfect program. There will always be a few bugs or problems. Debugging is all about solving problems and making the program as good as it can be.

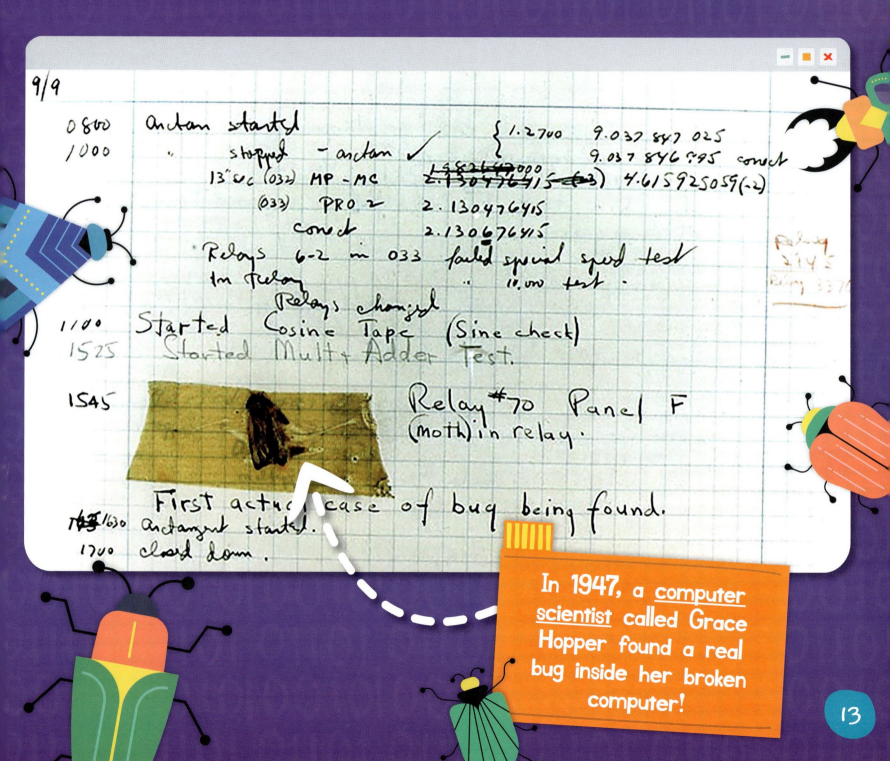

In 1947, a <u>computer scientist</u> called Grace Hopper found a real bug inside her broken computer!

PLAYING
AGAIN

It is important to test your code over and over again. You can get other people to test your code too. They can tell you if they find your program doing anything wrong.

The more people who test the code, the better!

```
integer euclidAlgorithm (int A, int
B){
     A=Math.abs(A);
     B=Math.abs(B);
     while (B!=0){
          if (A>B) A=A-B;
          else B=B-A;
     }
     return A;
}
integer euclidAlgorithm (int A, int
B){
     A=Math.abs(A);
     B=Math.abs(B);
     while (B!=0){
          if (A>B) A=A-B;
          else B=B-A;
     }
     return A;
}
integer euclidAlgorithm (int A, int
B){
     A=Math.abs(A);
     B=Math.abs(B);
     while (B!=0){
          if (A>B) A=A-B;
          else B=B-A;
     }
     return A;
}
```

People often test games again and again. This is called playtesting. If something goes wrong or doesn't work very well, they tell the programmer. The programmer then changes the code.

Someone who tests games is called a playtester.

GETTING IT Wrong

Here are some **common** bugs and mistakes in code:

There might be a spelling error.

Instructions might be in the wrong order.

There might be missing instructions.

The instructions might be impossible for the computer to do.

/《Fullo instruchions the all mon___?/ (4)

Meet Baboolean. The code monkeys have been writing code for her. But look at this messy code! There are lots of bugs!

BATHTIME FOR BABOOLEAN
> Appear next to bath (Baboolean can't appear!)
> Turn taps off when bath is ___ (missing step) (wrong order!)
> Turn taps on
> Add bubbles
> Add toys
> Get in baff (spelling mistake)

TiDY Monkeys

It is important that programmers keep their code neat and tidy. This way, it will be easier to read later and easier to find bugs.

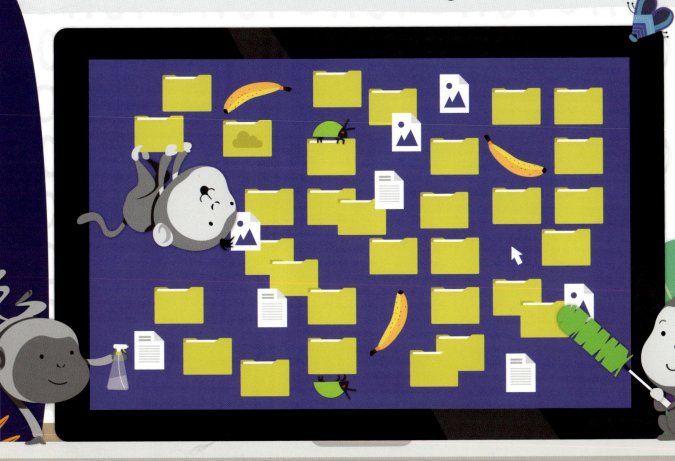

Programmers also leave comments in their code. These comments aren't read by the computer – they are there to let programmers know what is going on in the code.

```
# This code makes Baboolean say
"ooh ooh ah ah" five times.

for loop in range (5):
    print ("ooh ooh ah ah")
```

Computers know not to read the comments because the programmer marks them with symbols such as # or //. Different programming languages use different symbols.

"ooh ooh ah ah
ooh ooh ah ah
ooh ooh ah ah
ooh ooh ah ah
ooh ooh ah ah"

Monkey See

Here are some real bits of code that the monkeys have been writing. Oh dear – look at all the bugs.

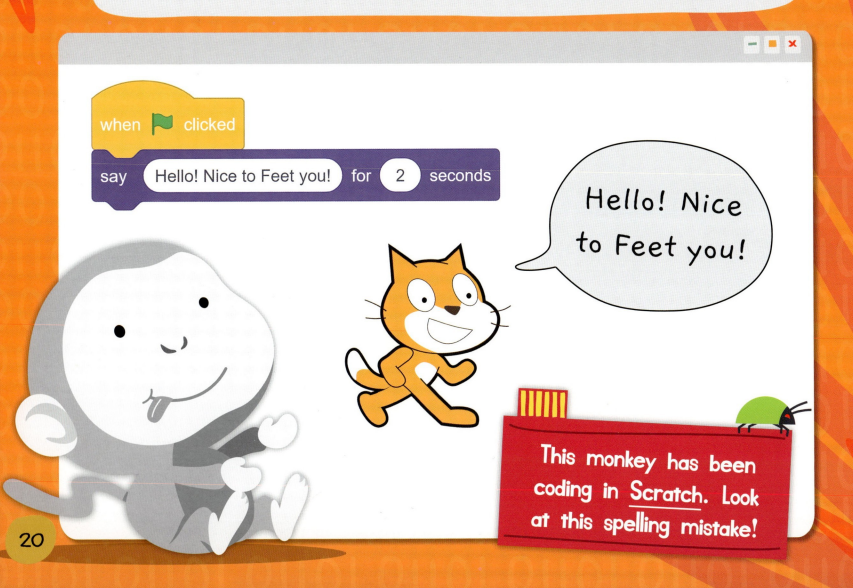

when 🚩 clicked

say Hello! Nice to Feet you! for 2 seconds

Hello! Nice to Feet you!

This monkey has been coding in <u>Scratch</u>. Look at this spelling mistake!

This monkey has been coding in **JavaScript**. In JavaScript, any opening brackets like (need to have closing brackets like) in the right place. But this monkey has forgotten to put closing brackets here! This code won't work.

```
<!DOCTYPE html>
<html>
<head>
        <title> Food Fight </title>
<script>
function foodFight() {
        var monkeys = 6
        var bananas = 5;
        if (monkeys > bananas      { alert("Food Fight!"); } }
foodFight();
</script>
</head>
</html>
```

Don't worry if this looks **complicated** – all you need to know is that code can't have a single tiny mistake in it, otherwise there will be bugs.

Monkey Do

Look at these two sets of instructions for Baboolean. Can you spot any mistakes? The answers are on page 23.

HOW TO HANG FROM A TREE

Z: Climb tree

2: Take your hands and feet off the branch

3: Hang upside down and wrap tail around branch

4: Hang by tayul

HOW TO CLEAN YOUR MONKEY FRIEND

1: Find monkey friend

2: Look for creepy crawly bug in monkey friend's fur

3: Sit next to monkey friend

4: Grab creepy crawly bug with ears

5: Put creepy crawly bug ⬜⬜⬜ and chew

6: Swallow creepy crawly bug

7: Burp

in mouth

Answers

HOW TO HANG FROM A TREE
2 instead of a 1
Swap round 2 and 3
Tail is spelt wrong in step 4

HOW TO CLEAN YOUR
MONKEY FRIEND
Swap 2 and 3 round
4 is impossible – change ears to fingers
'in mouth' is missing from step 5

23

Glossary

behaves	acts
common	often found or regularly occurring
complicated	made of many different parts and therefore hard to understand
computer scientist	someone who studies how computers are made and how they work
crash	(in computers) when a program stops working
instructions	a set of steps that explain how something is done
JavaScript	a type of programming language that is good for building websites
programming languages	languages that humans use to write instructions for computers
programs	sets of instructions that a computer is given to do different tasks
Scratch	a type of programming language made up of pictures and words – good for learning coding

Index